100% UNOFFICIAL

# ONE DREAM,
# ONE DIRECTION

# EDITED BY PHILIPPA WINGATE
# DESIGNED BY ZOE BRADLEY

## ALADDIN

An imprint of Simon & Schuster Children's Publishing Division
1230 Avenue of the Americas, New York, NY 10020
First Aladdin paperback edition July 2012
Text copyright © 2012 by Buster Books
Published by arrangement with Michael O'Mara Books Limited
Originally published in Great Britain in 2012 by Buster Books, an imprint of Michael O'Mara Books Limited
ALADDIN is a trademark of Simon & Schuster, Inc., and related logo is a registered trademark of Simon & Schuster, Inc.
For information about special discounts for bulk purchases, please contact Simon & Schuster Special Sales
at 1-866-506-1949 or business@simonandschuster.com.
The Simon & Schuster Speakers Bureau can bring authors to your live event. For more information or to book an event
contact the Simon & Schuster Speakers Bureau at 1-866-248-3049 or visit our website at www.simonspeakers.com.
Manufactured in the United States of America 0712 LAK
2 4 6 8 10 9 7 5 3
Library of Congress Control Number 2012939215
ISBN 978-1-4424-7308-9

PLEASE NOTE: This book is not affiliated with or endorsed by
One Direction or any of their publishers or licensees.

## PHOTO CREDITS

100% UNOFFICIAL

# ONE DREAM, ONE DIRECTION

BY ELLEN BAILEY (BUSTER BOOKS)   ALADDIN

# CONTENTS

# INTRODUCING THE FAB FIVE

The One Direction infection is spreading around the world. Have you got the bug? Symptoms include a high temperature, screaming, and sometimes even fainting. Oh, and there's no cure!

## THE BRITISH ARE COMING

Known as the "New British Invasion," Liam Payne, Zayn Malik, Niall Horan, Louis Tomlinson, and Harry Styles have introduced

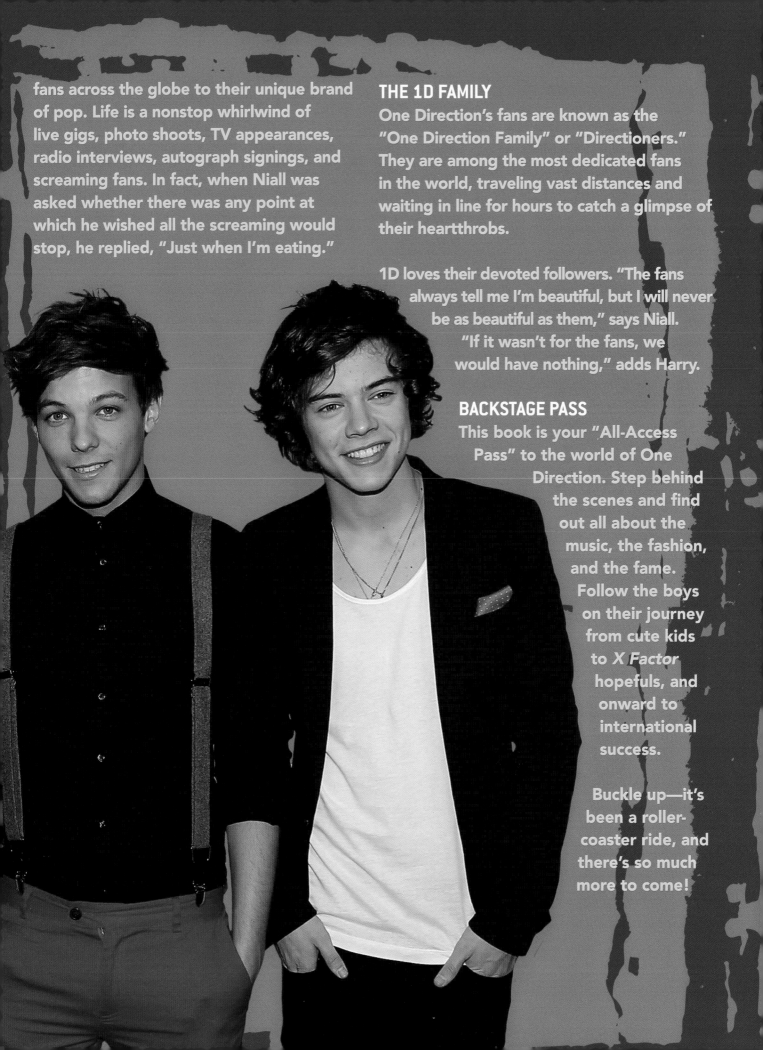

fans across the globe to their unique brand of pop. Life is a nonstop whirlwind of live gigs, photo shoots, TV appearances, radio interviews, autograph signings, and screaming fans. In fact, when Niall was asked whether there was any point at which he wished all the screaming would stop, he replied, "Just when I'm eating."

## THE 1D FAMILY

One Direction's fans are known as the "One Direction Family" or "Directioners." They are among the most dedicated fans in the world, traveling vast distances and waiting in line for hours to catch a glimpse of their heartthrobs.

1D loves their devoted followers. "The fans always tell me I'm beautiful, but I will never be as beautiful as them," says Niall. "If it wasn't for the fans, we would have nothing," adds Harry.

## BACKSTAGE PASS

This book is your "All-Access Pass" to the world of One Direction. Step behind the scenes and find out all about the music, the fashion, and the fame. Follow the boys on their journey from cute kids to *X Factor* hopefuls, and onward to international success.

Buckle up—it's been a roller-coaster ride, and there's so much more to come!

# HANDS UP FOR HARRY

## FACT FILE

**NAME:**
Harry Edward Styles

**DATE OF BIRTH:**
February 1, 1994

**STAR SIGN:**
Aquarius

**HOMETOWN:**
Holmes Chapel, Cheshire, England

**FAVORITE FILMS:**
*Love Actually* and *Titanic*

**FAVORITE COLORS:**
Pink and orange

***X FACTOR* AUDITION SONG:**
"Isn't She Lovely" by Stevie Wonder

**LIKES:**
Laser Quest and showers

**DISLIKES:**
Olives, swearing, and roller coasters

**CAN'T LIVE WITHOUT:**
L'Oréal Elvive shampoo and his phone

**CELEB CRUSH:**
Frankie from The Saturdays

**WOULD LIKE TO BE:**
Louis Tomlinson

**MOST LIKELY TO:**
Say what he thinks on live TV

**LEAST LIKELY TO:**
Straighten his hair

**KEY QUOTE:**
"I've always wanted to be one of those people who didn't really care that much about what people thought about them . . . but I just don't think I am."

**DID YOU KNOW?**
• Before he was in One Direction, Harry was the lead singer in a band called White Eskimo.

• When he met the rest of the fab five on *The X Factor*, it was Harry who came up with the name "One Direction."

# ZEALOUS FOR ZAYN

## FACT FILE

**NAME:**
Zayn Jawadd Malik

**DATE OF BIRTH:**
January 12, 1993

**STAR SIGN:**
Capricorn

**HOMETOWN:**
Bradford, England

**FAVORITE FILMS:**
*Scarface* and *Freedom Writers*

**FAVORITE COLORS:**
Red and blue

**X FACTOR AUDITION SONG:**
"Let Me Love You" by Mario

**LIKES:**
Sleeping in on Sundays, piercings, and scary movies

**DISLIKES:**
Pajamas, sandwich crusts, and swimming

**CAN'T LIVE WITHOUT:**
Mirrors or roast chicken

**CELEB CRUSH:**
Megan Fox

**WOULD LIKE TO BE:**
Justin Timberlake

**MOST LIKELY TO:**
Pout in a photo

**LEAST LIKELY TO:**
Be the first to finish getting ready in the morning

**KEY QUOTE:**
"Life is funny, things change, people change, but you will always be you, so stay true to yourself and never sacrifice who you are for anyone."

**DID YOU KNOW?**
• During *The X Factor*, Zayn was overcome with an attack of nerves and decided to remain backstage for a dance number. Simon Cowell noticed that Zayn was missing, went to find him, and convinced him to continue in the competition. Phew!

# LOUIS IS LUSH

## FACT FILE

**NAME:**
Louis William Tomlinson

**DATE OF BIRTH:**
December 24, 1991

**STAR SIGN:**
Capricorn

**HOMETOWN:**
Doncaster, South Yorkshire, England

**FAVORITE FILM:**
*Grease*

**FAVORITE COLORS:**
Purple and red

**X FACTOR AUDITION SONG:**
"Hey There Delilah" by Plain White T's

**LIKES:**
Sunbathing, silly voices, making people laugh, and computer games

**DISLIKES:**
Not having access to the Internet, being pale, and smoking

**CAN'T LIVE WITHOUT:**
His mom and dry shampoo—for when he can't be bothered to wash his hair

**CELEB CRUSHES:**
Emma Watson and Cheryl Cole

**WOULD LIKE TO BE:**
Robbie Williams

**MOST LIKELY TO:**
Play a practical joke on you

**LEAST LIKELY TO:**
Be serious in an interview

**KEY QUOTE:**
"Live life for the moment because everything else is uncertain."

**DID YOU KNOW?**
• Louis's mom has embarrassed him by telling baby stories on Twitter! His top three things to do as a kid were:
1. Sitting in his stroller and waving at everyone. 2. Climbing trees. 3. Making a "mix up" of cereals for breakfast. What a cutie!

# NO ONE'S LIKE NIALL

## FACT FILE

**NAME:**
Niall James Horan

**DATE OF BIRTH:**
September 13, 1993

**STAR SIGN:**
Virgo

**HOMETOWN:**
Mullingar, County Westmeath, Ireland

**FAVORITE FILMS:**
*Grease* and *The Godfather*

**FAVORITE COLORS:**
Yellow and blue

*X FACTOR* **AUDITION SONG:**
"So Sick" by Ne-Yo

**LIKES:**
Soccer, pizza, calling Simon Cowell
"Uncle Si"

**DISLIKES:**
Vegemite, clowns, and small spaces

**CAN'T LIVE WITHOUT:**
Sleep

**CELEB CRUSH:**
Cheryl Cole

**WOULD LIKE TO BE:**
Michael Bublé

**MOST LIKELY TO:**
Win you over with his Irish accent

**LEAST LIKELY TO:**
Use a cheesy pickup line or dye his blond
locks brown or black

**KEY QUOTE:**
"People think that a boy band is air
grabs and being dressed in all one color.
We're boys in a band. We're trying to do
something different from what people
would think is the typical kind of boy
band. We're trying to do different kinds
of music, and we're just trying to be
ourselves, not squeaky clean."

**DID YOU KNOW?**
• Niall could beat anyone in a farting
competition and can clear a room—or
a tour bus—in seconds!

# WE LOVE LIAM

## FACT FILE

**NAME:**
Liam James Payne

**DATE OF BIRTH:**
August 29, 1993

**STAR SIGN:**
Virgo

**HOMETOWN:**
Wolverhampton, West Midlands, England

**FAVORITE FILMS:**
The Toy Story films

**FAVORITE COLORS:**
Purple and blue

***X FACTOR* AUDITION SONG:**
"Cry Me a River" by Michael Bublé

**LIKES:**
Singing in the shower, surprises, hair straighteners, and massages

**DISLIKES:**
Nasty tweets, flying, and spoons

**CAN'T LIVE WITHOUT:**
Hair products

**CELEB CRUSH:**
Leona Lewis

**WOULD LIKE TO BE:**
Comedian Michael McIntyre

**MOST LIKELY TO:**
Ask you out on a date by serenading you

**LEAST LIKELY TO:**
Be rude

**KEY QUOTE:**
"I try to be cool, but I'm not very good at it."

**DID YOU KNOW?**
• Liam first auditioned for *The X Factor* in 2008 when he was just fourteen years old. He reached the Judges' Houses stage of the competition. But Simon Cowell said he thought Liam wasn't ready and asked him to come back two years later. We're so glad he did!

# FOREVER YOUNG

Before Liam, Harry, Zayn, Louis, and Niall came together to form One Direction, they were just five supercute kids with big ambitions. The boys may have dreamed of superstardom, but they could never have known what was just around the corner. . . .

## LIAM
"When I was little I always said that I wanted a brother. Now it's like having four of them."

Liam is proof that if you set your mind to something, you can achieve it, no matter what challenges come your way. Liam was born with only one working kidney, and as a young child he was in and out of the hospital all the time. He used to have to have thirty-two injections a day! Determined not to let his illness hold him back, Liam started getting up at six o'clock every morning and running for miles before school. His dedication paid off when he made his school's

under-18s cross-country team. He also took up boxing, which was great for deterring the school bullies: "It gave me confidence. I got pretty good over the next couple of years." That confidence certainly shines through in his cheeky grin.

## NIALL
**"All my family remember the fact that I was always singing something or other."**

Multitalented Niall has been impressing people with his musical abilities from an early age. He took up the guitar when he was just twelve, and started performing at live events. He entered—and won—a number of talent shows and knew that he was destined for a career as a performer.

Niall's parents, Maura and Bobby, split up when he was little, but came together during the *X Factor* competition, pulling out all the stops for their son. "It was a fantastic experience to watch my son perform live in front of all those people," says his dad, Bobby. "He did very well."

## HARRY
**"I had a few girlfriends here and there when I was really young, but I didn't have an actual girlfriend until I was twelve."**

Harry loved singing and dancing from an early age and laid down his first tracks when he was just a little kid. "My dad introduced me to his music, and when I got given a karaoke machine by my granddad, my cousin and I recorded a load of Elvis tracks." Harry is always ready for a laugh. "I used to moon a bit at school because it made me laugh!"

## LOUIS
**"I went through a seriously dodgy clothes phase when I was about thirteen."**

Louis grew up with four younger sisters: Charlotte, Félicité, and twins Daisy and Phoebe. "I suppose in some ways it taught me about women," says Louis. "Having that many sisters has definitely helped me with children, too . . . I absolutely love babies, and the boys are always [teasing] me for how broody I am."

Before he was in One Direction, Louis went to acting school and played parts in various TV shows, but he says that the best job he ever had was at a cinema, because he got to see all the latest films. He didn't take much interest in clothes until he was seventeen, but that's all changed now.

## ZAYN
**"I was a bit of a handful when I was a kid because I was quite hyperactive."**

Zayn's good looks come from his mixed cultural background—his mom is British and his dad is Pakistani. But it wasn't always easy being different from the other kids. "I almost felt like I didn't fit in at my first two schools," he remembers. "When my sister and I moved to a different school it was a lot more mixed, so I felt like I fit in better. Also, all of the girls wanted to know who this new kid was and that's when I became cool." Zayn experimented with different haircuts through his teens— he even shaved his head and had slits in his eyebrows! "I thought I was properly gangsta, being into R&B and rap."

# THE *X FACTOR* JOURNEY

It's been a roller-coaster ride to superstardom for the fab five. Back at the beginning of One Direction's journey, there were heart-stopping moments during their time on *The X Factor,* in 2010.

## HEADING HOME

Liam, Harry, Zayn, Louis, and Niall initially auditioned as solo artists, and each of them thought their dreams were over when they were told that they hadn't made it through to the next stage of the competition. But the judges decided that the teens were too talented to send home. When guest judge Nicole Scherzinger suggested that the five soloists join together to become a group act, history was in the making.

Simon Cowell recognized the lads' potential and mentored them through the rest of the competition. Simon is known for his ability to spot true talent, and the boys have proved he wasn't wrong to rate them so highly.

## AN UNBREAKABLE BOND

Together, the boys were unstoppable. In no time at all they had formed a strong friendship, an unbreakable bond, and a unique sound. The other more established bands in the competition didn't stand a chance as, week by week, the boys won

over both the judges and TV audiences with their renditions of hit songs. Here's a guide to the songs they sang onstage during the live shows:

Week One: "Viva La Vida"
Week Two: "My Life Would Suck Without You"
Week Three: "Nobody Knows"
Week Four: "Total Eclipse of the Heart"

Week Five: "Kids in America"
Week Six: "The Way You Look Tonight"
Week Seven: "All You Need Is Love"
Week Eight: "You Are So Beautiful" and "Summer of '69"
Week Nine: "Chasing Cars" and "Only Girl (In the World)"

One Direction made it to the live grand finale of *The X Factor* and eventually finished third, close behind Rebecca Ferguson and the winner, Matt Cardle. For some performers this would have been the end of their story, but not for 1D.

### SIGNED UP
Fans everywhere went wild when One Direction's version of "Forever Young," the song that they would have released had they won the competition, was leaked on the Internet. Simon Cowell immediately signed the boys to his record label Syco, and the whirlwind of life as an international boy band began.

### THE REST IS HISTORY
After the season finished, the boys joined their fellow contestants again and embarked on the *X Factor* tour, delighting fans all over the UK.

From their humble beginnings on *The X Factor,* there's now only one direction that Harry, Louis, Zayn, Liam, and Niall are headed in, and that's up to the stars!

# GETTING TO KNOW YOU

After the boys were thrown together on *The X Factor*, it didn't take long for them to become fast friends. In no time at all they were as close as any boy band on the planet, and, we think you will agree, their bond is reflected in their perfect harmonies.

## MAKING IT WORK

Liam, Harry, Zayn, Louis, and Niall each bring something unique to the group, but when you put five talented and opinionated boys together, it can take some work to make sure everyone feels that his voice is being heard. "At the start all our ideas were

clashing a bit," admits Zayn. "It's been kind of hard to start off with because we were all thrown together," says Liam. "We had such a short space of time to get to know each other. But we all get along so well and we're all living together now and it's amazing!"

## PRACTICAL JOKERS
Both in the *X Factor* house and on tour the boys have bonded in the way most guys do—they play practical jokes on each

other! They took to creeping into each other's bedrooms and attacking each other with hair clippers. "Liam was asleep and Zayn shaved a slit in his eyebrow," reveals Harry. "Then Zayn was asleep, and I shaved my initials into his leg hair."

Louis likes to play tricks too. "Grrr! Louis regularly breaks into my room and throws buckets of water over me when I'm sleeping," complains Niall.

With all these pranks going on, it's no wonder Harry sometimes finds himself missing home. In the *X Factor* house he confessed, "The house is always pretty loud. You have your messy people and your tidy people, but it's really good living with all the boys. I miss my mum a little bit, though."

## DOWN TO BUSINESS
The boys certainly know how to have a good time, but you don't get to be an international pop sensation without some seriously hard work. These professionals know when it's time to stop messing around and get down to business.

"I think that, socially, having spent so much time together we have become really good friends," explains Harry. "But when it comes down to the performances and the rehearsing, we are professional and we don't let it get in the way. We are business when we need to be."

# SHOOT FOR THE STARS

Is your future with your favorite member of One Direction written in the stars? Read on to find out.

If your star sign is Gemini, Libra, Sagittarius, Aries, or Aquarius, then your astrological love match is . . .

**HARRY**

If your star sign is Leo, Capricorn, or Cancer, then your love matches are . . .

**LIAM AND NIALL**

If your star sign is Taurus, Virgo, Scorpio, or Pisces, then your astrological love matches are . . .

**ZAYN AND LOUIS**

Harry is an **Aquarius**, which means he's open-minded and likes to explore new horizons. **Aquarians** love smart girls who are good conversationalists— you might be the prettiest girl in the world, but if you can't engage his mind, then he just won't be interested. **Aquarians** need freedom and hate it when girls get jealous. But there's no need to worry— **Aquarians** make loyal boyfriends.

**QUALITIES:** Friendly, independent, honest

**LIKES:** Dreaming of the future and remembering the past

**DISLIKES:** People being fake or two-faced

**BIRTHSTONE:** Amethyst

**LUCKY COLOR:** Blue

**LUCKY DAY:** Sunday

Both Liam and Niall are Virgos, which means they are cool and calm on the outside, but full of emotion on the inside. If these boys play it cool at the beginning of a relationship, then you know why. Virgos like to feel safe and go for girls who aren't too impulsive or unconventional. Virgos make great boyfriends because they will stand by you no matter what.

**QUALITIES:** Intelligent, modest, practical, witty

**LIKES:** Precision, cleanliness, order

**DISLIKES:** Sloppy work, uncertainty

**BIRTHSTONE:** Sapphire

**LUCKY COLOR:** Green

**LUCKY DAY:** Wednesday

Zayn and Louis are **Capricorns**, which suggests that they are very physical and passionate. It takes **Capricorns** a long time to trust people, so any girls they date need to be prepared to take it slow at the beginning of the relationship and not expect too much too soon. Once you've unlocked their hearts, however, they'll be yours forever.

**QUALITIES:** Ambitious, patient, stable

**LIKES:** Privacy, home, and family

**DISLIKES:** Being lonely, being teased

**BIRTHSTONE:** Garnet

**LUCKY COLOR:** Brown

**LUCKY DAY:** Saturday

# IT'S GOT TO BE YOU

Liam, Harry, Louis, Zayn, and Niall have never had any trouble finding a date, and since becoming famous there are hundreds of thousands of girls who would do just about anything to meet them.

Here's your chance to ponder what the One Direction boys look for in a girl. What would they be like in a relationship if all your dreams really did come true?

| ♡ | LIAM | HARRY | ZAYN | NIALL | LOUIS |
|---|---|---|---|---|---|
| AS A BOYFRIEND HE IS | loyal and faithful | faithful and fun | shy at first | always up for a laugh | loyal and trustworthy |
| GET HIS ATTENTION BY | flashing him a big smile | flicking your hair | paying him a compliment | wearing a pair of hot pants | telling him a joke |
| HE LIKES GIRLS WHO | have brown hair | are older than him | play it cool | can handle being teased | are clean and tidy |
| HE DOESN'T LIKE GIRLS WHO | are too over the top | squeal | are clingy | are into Disney films | have tattoos |
| EXPECT HIM TO TURN UP FOR A DATE IN | jeans and a T-shirt | jeans, a nice top, and a blazer | jeans and a T-shirt | jeans, a shirt, and a blazer | chinos and a polo shirt |

# IT'S ALL IN A NAME

Do you need to know which of the One Direction boys is right for you? Find out if the answer is in your name. . . .

1. Count the number of letters in your first name, and add it to the number of letters in your surname.

2. Divide this number by two. If you end up with a half number, round it up. For example if you get 5.5, round it up to 6.

3. Starting at the top heart with Harry's name in it, count around the flower petals until you reach your number, then color in that heart.

4. Continue counting on the following uncolored hearts, skipping any that are already colored in. Every time you reach your number, color in that heart.

5. When there is only one heart left uncolored, that's your boy!

# CHART TOPPERS

Since being signed to Simon Cowell's label, Syco, One Direction has been rocketing up the charts all over the globe. Here's exactly what they have been up to. . . .

**FEBRUARY 2011:** The boys head off on the *X Factor* tour of the United Kingdom.

**APRIL 2011:** One Direction is announced as the stars of a series of ads for Pokémon Black and Pokémon White on Nintendo DS and Nintendo DSi.

**MAY 2011:** The boys head to Sweden to start work in the studio and record their first single. "When the demo came through for 'What Makes You Beautiful' we instantly felt good about it," says Louis.

**JULY 2011:** 1D heads to Los Angeles to shoot the video for "What Makes You Beautiful." They also celebrate their one-year anniversary as a band.

**SEPTEMBER 2011:** The single breaks preorder sales records for Sony Music, and enters the UK Singles Chart at number one, selling 153,965 copies in the first week.

**SEPTEMBER 2011:** The boys publish their first book,

*Dare to Dream*, and tour the UK, attending sold-out book signings.

**OCTOBER 2011:** Directioners all over the world campaign for the band to visit them in the "Bring 1D to Me" challenge. The boys visit Sweden, Italy, Holland, and Germany.

**NOVEMBER 2011:** The boys' second single, "Gotta Be You," and their first album, *Up All Night*, are released in the UK.

The album becomes 2011's fastest-selling debut album.

**DECEMBER 2011:** The boys tour the UK. Tickets sell out within minutes.

**FEBRUARY 2012:** One Direction releases their third single, "One Thing."

**MARCH 2012:** 1D becomes the first British group in history to reach number one in the US Billboard chart with their debut album. "We simply cannot believe that we are No. 1 in America! It's beyond a dream come true for us," exclaims Harry.

**APRIL 2012:** The boys sell over 4 million albums in six months. They head to America and Australia to perform and promote their album, and are number one in more than fourteen countries.

**MAY/JUNE 2012:** One Direction heads stateside again for their big North American tour, playing in huge venues across the country and meeting their American fans face-to-face.

# THE 1D FAMILY

Directioners are among the most devoted fans around. If you know the words to all their songs, follow the boys on Facebook and Twitter, have posters of the band all over your bedroom walls, and would travel miles just to catch a glimpse of them, then you can consider yourself part of the 1D family. And what a family it is. . . .

## WHAT KIND OF FAN ARE YOU?

According to One Direction, there are a few different types of fan. There are the fans who scream, swoon, and maybe even pass out. Then there are the ones who play it cool and chat with the boys. Finally, there are the shy fans, who prefer to admire the gorgeous guys from a distance. Only you know which kind of fan you are.

## ONE DIRECTION ON THEIR FANS

Here are some of the things the boys have said about their much-loved admirers:

• "We would be nowhere without our incredible fans—we owe it all to you." (Louis)

• "I don't think you should ever date someone or not based on whether they're a fan—if they're a fan then that's cool." (Zayn)

• "A couple of fans asked us to sign their big toenails. It wasn't that gross, it was okay. I guess there are worse places to sign." (Harry)

## STRANGE GIFTS

The boys have received some pretty weird and wonderful presents from their fans. Here are some of the strangest:

Harry—a lettuce
Niall—a real-live baby lamb
Liam—a box of mushrooms
Louis—a sack of carrots
Zayn—a Borat-style mankini

## TOTALLY DEVOTED

One Direction fans really do go the extra mile for their heroes. Here are some of the most extraordinary acts of devotion they have performed for their idols:

• One seventeen-year-old shaved her head to win tickets to a sold-out One Direction show and to raise money for *Leukaemia & Blood Cancer New Zealand*. She donated her hair to make a wig for someone with cancer. That's true love!

• Over three hundred Canadian superfans camped out for thirty-five hours in the freezing cold to catch a glimpse of their heartthrobs in Montreal. Temperatures outside the venue dropped as low as –10° C (14° F). Fan frrrrrrrenzy!

• Groups of fans have been dressing up as the band. "In Boston we did a meet and greet and these five girls came dressed as each of us," remembers Harry. "They do that a lot. It's cool."

# BEHIND THE SCENES

Have you ever wondered what the One Direction boys really get up to when the cameras are off? They would tell you that touring is like being at one giant sleepover with your four best friends, interspersed with performing to crowds of screaming fans, red-carpet appearances, and photo shoots.

Jump on the tour bus and find out what life is really like when One Direction hits the road.

## SOCCER STARS

To keep themselves amused on the tour bus, especially when they're traveling long distances, One Direction loves to play a soccer game called FIFA on their game consoles. They have tournaments to see who's the champion.

As soon as the bus pulls over and the boys have a chance to stretch their legs, it's a race to have a real kick around. The boys are athletic and love soccer—it's the perfect way to wind down and relax.

## COUNTING THEIR BLESSINGS

The down-to-earth boys know how lucky they are to do what they love and wake up in a new city every day. "People our age are normally in school and stuff like that," says Harry. "We get to travel around the world. Look out there—it's New York!"

## ROAD TRIP RULES

According to the boys, there are five key rules to successfully sharing a tour bus:
1. Clean up after yourself.
2. Sleep when you want.
3. Eat a lot.
4. Don't let any girls on the bus.
5. Always let Niall have the top bunk.

## PRANKSTERS

The boys love to get up to mischief and play pranks on each other to pass the time. Who do you think comes out on top in the prankster chart?

• Louis, for sticking straws up Harry's nose while he's asleep to make him look like a walrus.

• Liam, for throwing a bucket of water over Niall while he's asleep.

• Harry, for putting gaffer tape over Louis's mouth, then ripping it off.

• Zayn, for spraying Niall in the face with a fire extinguisher.

• Niall, for taking a photo of Liam on the toilet.

# ROAD TRIP!

**START:**
NEW YORK CITY

YOUR FRIENDS ARE SO JEALOUS! TO AVOID THEIR CRAZY SOUVENIR REQUESTS, MOVE FORWARD 3 SPACES.

The One Direction boys have finished their tour and are heading off on a road trip, making their way from the hustle and bustle of New York City to the sun and surf in laid-back Los Angeles for a party on the beach. And the best news is—you're invited!

Grab a die, find a friend, and play this game to see which one of you can get to the beach party first.

YOU AND THE BOYS ARE BEING CHASED BY THE PAPARAZZI. JUMP FORWARD 1 SPACE TO LOSE THEM.

YOU'VE OVERSLEPT AND THE 1D BOYS HAVE LEFT WITHOUT YOU. MISS A TURN.

**TIME-OUT ZONE:**
ROLL A 6 TO GET OUT.

YOU LEFT YOUR BACKSTAGE PASS IN NEW YORK. HEAD TO THE "TIME-OUT ZONE."

A REPORTER GRILLS YOU FOR SECRETS, AND BY MISTAKE YOU SPILL. MOVE BACK 4 SPACES.

ON A GLAMOROUS SHOPPING SPREE WITH THE 1D STYLIST, YOU LOSE TRACK OF TIME. MOVE BACK 1 SPACE.

LAST-MINUTE STAGE FRIGHT. MISS A TURN.

**FINISH:** BEACH PARTY CENTRAL

YOU ARE INVITED TO AN A-LIST PARTY! ROLL AGAIN.

YOU'VE BEEN SNAPPED BY PAPS OUT WITH THE BOYS, AND EVERYONE'S TALKING ABOUT YOU. MOVE BACK 2 SPACES.

THE BOYS ASK YOU TO APPEAR IN THEIR NEXT VIDEO! MOVE FORWARD 2 SPACES.

# SO STYLISH

One Direction certainly knows how to cut it style-wise. They've been spotted in the front row at London Fashion Week, they were nominated for *GQ* magazine's Best Dressed Award 2012, and superstars have been caught stealing their style! Whether they're dressing up in suits for a red-carpet appearance or dressing down in shorts for the beach, the boys always manage to look effortlessly cool. Here's how. . . .

## STAYING TRUE TO THEIR ROOTS

Liam, Zayn, Niall, Harry, and Louis say that, since becoming famous, they have all gained confidence in their own sense of style and encourage each other to express themselves through their clothes.

Their look has developed since they first became One Direction, but their secret to looking good is that they've remained true to their own unique sense of style. Zayn is the edgiest and takes his fashion very seriously. Louis loves a relaxed, nautical look. Harry likes to look sharp in tailored suits. For Liam, comfort's the most important thing—he loves to relax in lumberjack shirts and jeans, and Niall likes to chill in jeans and polo shirts in pale, neutral shades.

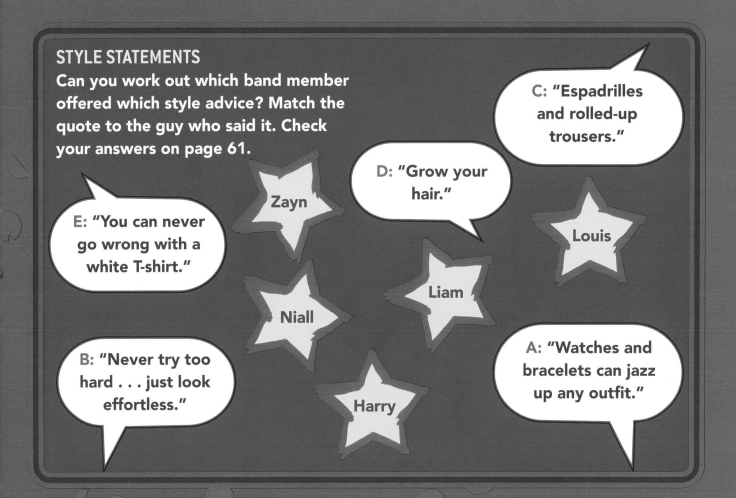

## STYLE STATEMENTS
Can you work out which band member offered which style advice? Match the quote to the guy who said it. Check your answers on page 61.

C: "Espadrilles and rolled-up trousers."

D: "Grow your hair."

Zayn

Louis

E: "You can never go wrong with a white T-shirt."

Liam

Niall

B: "Never try too hard . . . just look effortless."

A: "Watches and bracelets can jazz up any outfit."

Harry

## BREAKING THE RULES
The One Direction boys aren't afraid to break a few fashion rules. They love to mix and match formal styles with more relaxed, classic pieces. It's not everyone who can pull off a pinstriped suit with high-top sneakers, or a bow tie and skinny jeans, but these stylish guys certainly know how to put a look together.

## BRAND MAGNETS
One of the best things about being in 1D is that famous clothing labels send them free stuff. The boys favor sporty labels such as Bench, Caterpillar, and G-Star Raw. Niall loves Fred Perry tennis shoes, Nike Dunks, and Converse sneakers. Liam likes to hang out in Jack Wills between shows, and some of Harry's favorite outfits come from designer brand Aquascutum.

## ONE FOR ONE
Louis is a massive fan of the ethical brand TOMS and often wears one of his many pairs of TOMS shoes. TOMS was founded by Blake Mycoskie, an American who, while traveling in Argentina, came across children who had no shoes to protect their feet. Blake came up with the idea of the One for One Movement—for every pair of shoes purchased, a pair of new shoes is given to a child in need. In this way the 1D boys have helped loads of children in developing countries, and have looked good while they've done it.

## DID YOU KNOW?
• Never ones to take themselves too seriously, the boys love to hang out in one-piece jumpsuits. All-in-One Direction, anyone?

# WHO'S THE ONE FOR YOU?

Are you made for Zayn, perfect for Harry, or ideal for Liam? Do you want to be Niall's girl or Louis's lady? Follow this flow chart to work out which of the 1D boys you're most compatible with. . . .

A sophisticated sister.

Play it cool.

**4. How would your friends describe you?**

A funny bunny.

Take a back seat.

**2. You see the boy you like at a party. What do you do?**

Rush home to change.

**1. Your friends suggest playing a practical joke on a teacher. What do you do?**

Talk to him.

**5. In the middle of the school day you spill a bright red drink down your top.**

Make her a gift.

Declare it's a new look.

Spring into action.

**3. Your best friend is feeling down. How do you cheer her up?**

Roll your eyes.

**6. A boy uses a cheesy pickup line on you. What do you do?**

Tell her a joke.

Say one right back.

Go for a run.

Liam

7. You're feeling stressed. How do you let off steam?

Take a long shower.

Zayne

Hide indoors.

8. You wake up with a giant zit on your face. What do you do?

Go out anyway.

Niall

Be nice.

9. An interviewer asks you what you think of Simon Cowell's sense of style. You think it's terrible! What do you do?

Harry

Tell the truth.

Run and hide.

10. Your friend's mom asks you to babysit her three little children. What do you do?

Louis

Jump at the chance.

# TELL ME A LIE

Here are a dozen statements about One Direction. Can you work out which of them are true and which are false? Check your answers on page 61.

**STATEMENT ONE:**
Louis was stung by a sea urchin during the Judges' Houses round of The X Factor.

**STATEMENT FOUR:**
One Direction likes to hang out with a pigeon named Kevin.

**STATEMENT THREE:**
Zayn is half Spanish.

**STATEMENT SEVEN:**
Liam has a birthmark on his neck.

**STATEMENT TWO:**
Niall loves mayonnaise.

**STATEMENT SIX:**
"Gotta Be You" is the first track on the album Up All Night.

**STATEMENT FIVE:**
Harry has an older sister.

**STATEMENT TEN:**
The boys made prank calls to Simon Cowell.

**STATEMENT NINE:**
Louis calls Niall a human trash can because he eats so much.

**STATEMENT EIGHT:**
Niall's mom once auditioned for The X Factor.

**STATEMENT TWELVE:**
Harry went to the same school as Kate Middleton, who is now the Duchess of Cambridge.

**STATEMENT ELEVEN:**
Zayn and Niall were in a TV ad for Levi's jeans.

# HEADING STATESIDE

One Direction totally loved their first American adventure. They were greeted at the Los Angeles airport by an army of fans waving signs and the boys knew instantly that it was going to be the trip of a lifetime. From there, it was a nonstop whirlwind of movie premieres, sold-out signings, and live shows. Find out what they got up to. . . .

## FAN-TASTIC
One Direction wasn't expecting anything like the reception that they received in America. "You see quite a few names on Twitter—people saying 'I'm from America! I'm from America!'" says Louis. "But until you're here, and you see it, it doesn't really seem real."

According to the boys, the US fans are the loudest, craziest, and most confident in the world. They love how American fans aren't afraid to come up and talk to them, and have been overwhelmed by how much love they've received from their stateside fans!

## BIG TIME RUSH
One Direction supported American boy band Big Time Rush on their tour of the states, and both bands had a blast both onstage and offstage. "The Big Time Rush boys are actually a lot like us," says Liam. "They're kind of mischievous and like to have a lot of fun. We're very similar." One Direction's popularity exploded as the tour went on, and they were invited to perform at Nickelodeon's 25th Annual Kids' Choice Awards in Los Angeles. This was a huge honor for the five British boys, and they were especially excited to meet Katy Perry, Will Smith, and David Beckham, and they were even introduced to the First Lady, Michelle Obama, backstage.

## iCARLY
During their time in the US, 1D made a guest appearance on the sitcom *iCarly*. This gave them a chance to show off their acting skills on American TV. In the episode, Harry tries to get Carly's attention by pretending to be sick. To persuade him to get out of bed again, the boys come up with a plan to make Harry think that Carly's friend Gibby is taking his place in One Direction.

The plan works and Harry gets up to perform "What Makes You Beautiful" with the band. It was a seriously good show!

## MAD FOR MADISON

One Direction may have made history when their debut album reached number one in the US charts, but the boys knew they'd really made it in the States when they sold out Madison Square Garden—the third-biggest venue in the world—in just one hour.

Liam thanked fans on Twitter, "I cannot wait it's going to be the most amazing night ever. Thank you so much for helping us sell out Madison Square Gardens!!!! :)x" Louis's mom even got in on the action and tweeted, "So the boys broke YET another record :) #properband #proudmummy X."

## FIRST LADY

The boys were amazed to receive an invitation to an Easter egg hunt at the White House. They were devastated when they had to decline because they were due to be on tour in Australia.

## THE BIG TOUR

One Direction's passion for heading stateside was confirmed when they announced a North American tour playing in venues all over the country in May and June 2012.

One Direction's American love affair is setting everyone's hearts aflutter!

# WORD SEARCH

The titles of all the songs on 1D's first album are hidden in this word search. Can you find them all? The words might run up, down, forward, backward, or diagonally. Check your answers on page 61.

| U | O | D | J | U | P | E | F | L | W | I | E | D | E | L | B | A | N | O | W | L |
| O | S | E | K | A | G | N | I | H | T | E | N | O | M | T | A | H | T | K | U | A |
| Y | O | U | B | E | A | I | W | A | N | T | U | T | I | S | F | U | L | F | O | R |
| T | N | R | E | T | S | A | I | E | T | A | E | R | T | G | R | E | I | B | E | S |
| U | S | T | M | I | L | L | S | R | E | A | D | O | C | A | M | T | B | S | R | A |
| O | O | E | R | V | O | R | H | G | S | T | L | E | R | R | U | A | B | A | I | V |
| B | E | R | Y | A | V | E | N | T | I | E | L | U | P | A | P | R | I | M | D | E |
| A | G | A | G | U | V | B | R | O | M | F | Y | A | E | M | A | L | S | E | G | Y |
| G | B | O | L | I | N | G | S | Y | T | R | A | B | Y | J | L | S | B | M | E | O |
| N | A | J | T | E | C | N | H | E | N | E | U | S | N | A | L | Y | T | I | A | U |
| I | M | I | E | T | B | E | A | K | E | O | R | J | A | C | N | K | I | S | E | T |
| H | H | A | M | E | A | E | D | I | Y | R | M | P | S | N | I | L | O | T | C | O |
| T | U | C | K | R | L | B | E | S | B | E | R | Y | F | I | G | N | W | A | H | N |
| Y | O | H | T | C | S | T | E | A | Y | O | U | T | N | E | H | R | A | K | Y | I |
| R | O | L | M | R | G | K | A | Y | T | E | S | P | A | R | T | A | K | E | N | G |
| E | G | L | O | C | A | Y | T | I | O | N | U | M | O | C | E | D | O | S | K | H |
| V | L | O | N | M | G | R | D | S | I | U | X | T | F | O | R | T | T | A | B | T |
| E | I | Y | T | E | L | L | M | E | A | L | I | E | A | D | R | E | S | E | Y | E |
| W | E | A | N | T | O | S | E | E | M | A | S | T | S | A | M | E | V | E | T | O |
| I | H | M | A | E | K | Z | W | S | I | H | T | N | A | H | T | E | R | O | M | N |
| W | M | E | S | N | A | T | Q | J | K | L | B | T | R | A | E | N | T | H | G | I |

**MORE THAN THIS**   ONE THING   I WISH   I WANT   **SAVE YOU TONIGHT**

GOTTA BE YOU   **UP ALL NIGHT**   SAME MISTAKES   STOLE MY HEART

WHAT MAKES YOU BEAUTIFUL   TELL ME A LIE   **TAKEN**   EVERYTHING ABOUT YOU

# THEIR NUMBER ONE FAN

Put your superfan status to the test with this 1D quiz. Check your answers on page 61.

Every time you get an answer right, shade in a star on the right-hand side of the page, starting at the bottom. The closer you get to the big star at the top, the higher your superfan status!

**1. What name did Zayn originally suggest for the band?**

A: New Direction
B: *Pente*—which sounds like the Greek word for "five"
C: The Zaynorators

**2. Which member of One Direction first appeared on *The X Factor* in 2008, and made it through to the Judges' Houses round?**

A: Liam
B: Zayn
C: Harry

**3. For what event was One Direction invited to the White House?**

A: The birthday of President Obama's daughter, Malia
B: Thanksgiving Dinner
C: An Easter egg hunt

**4. Which of the following books has Niall read?**

A: *To Kill a Mockingbird*
B: *Lord of the Flies*
C: *Of Mice and Men*

**5. Which member of One Direction has four sisters?**

A: Louis
B: Harry
C: Liam

**6. What is Harry's middle name?**

A: James
B: Edward
C: Arthur

**7. Who is the oldest member of One Direction?**

A: Liam
B: Niall
C: Louis

**8. What is Liam's Twitter ID?**

A: @Real_Liam_Payne
B: @LiamOfficial
C: @liampayne

**9. In which three places was the album *Up All Night* recorded?**

A: The UK, Italy, and the US
B: The UK, Sweden, and the US
C: Sweden, the US, and France

**10. Which of the following is Niall's lucky mascot?**

A: A pair of white socks
B: A white leather bracelet
C: A white polo shirt

**11. Which unusual instrument does Harry play?**

A: The keytar
B: The bazantar
C: The kazoo

**12. Who sings the most solos on the album *Up All Night*?**

A: Harry
B: Zayn
C: Liam

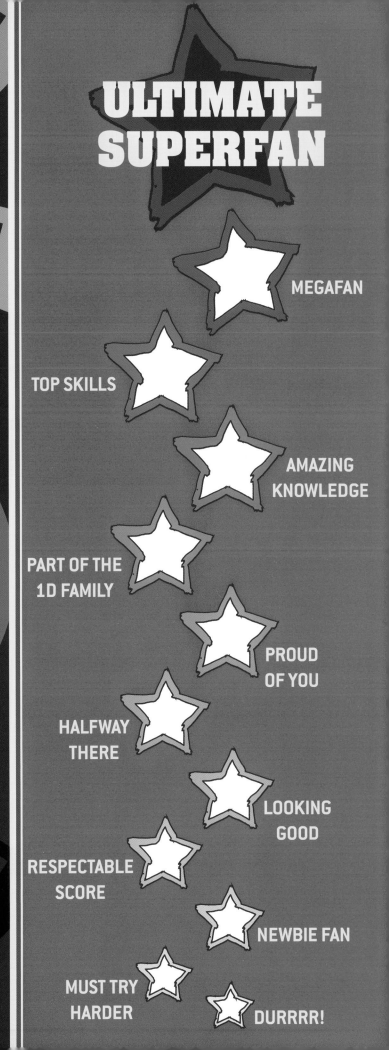

# ULTIMATE SUPERFAN

MEGAFAN

TOP SKILLS

AMAZING KNOWLEDGE

PART OF THE 1D FAMILY

PROUD OF YOU

HALFWAY THERE

LOOKING GOOD

RESPECTABLE SCORE

NEWBIE FAN

MUST TRY HARDER

DURRRR!

# THE FUTURE'S BRIGHT

It would be hard to top the year that Liam, Zayn, Harry, Niall, and Louis have just had. How do you beat a meteoric rise to international superstardom?

It looks like the coming year is going to be just as full of number one hits, award ceremonies, and, of course, screaming fans! There's no stopping these boys now. Here's what's already on their schedule.

## SOPHOMORE ALBUM

One Direction is already working on their second album, and it's set to be just as huge as the first! The boys, who helped write some of the songs on *Up All Night*, are eager to work with the best and brightest stars in the music business.

Simon Cowell has challenged the world's greatest songwriters and producers to work with One Direction to pen their next smash hit. Already confirmed to collaborate on the album are talents such as Rami Yacoub, Carl Falk and Savan Kotecha—who cowrote "What Makes You Beautiful"—Tom Fletcher from McFly, and

Max Martin and Kristian Lundin, who is famous for hits recorded by Britney Spears, Katy Perry, and Pink. There are also rumors that Adele might be involved.

## STADIUM TOUR

Following their amazing North American tour, One Direction is scheduled to play their first-ever stadium tour in 2013. The tour will take in the biggest and best venues in the UK, giving thousands of British fans the chance to see the boys on their home soil. A worldwide tour is likely to follow, so that Directioners all over the globe can get in on the action.

## LIVING THE DREAM

The boys loved working on their first book, *Dare to Dream*, and are set to publish another title in 2013. The book will chart their rise to fame across the globe, and it promises to be packed with unseen behind-the-scenes photos and gossip to help fans get a feel for who the boys really are. "We . . . hope to give the fans something new and special," says Niall. "For us, the most important thing is that our fans love and are happy with anything we put out. . . . We can't wait to get working on it."

# IN IT TO WIN IT

It isn't just the fans who are devoted to One Direction—the entire music industry has been lining up to recognize the band's achievements. Here's what the boys' awards collection looks like.

**DID YOU KNOW?**
The One Direction boys aren't afraid to share the limelight. They nominated their writers and producers Rami Yacoub, Carl Flak, and Savan Kotecha for an Unsung Heroes Brit Award 2012. The award celebrates the people who work behind the scenes in the music industry.

**2011 J-14 Teen Icon Awards**

Icon of Tomorrow
WINNERS

**2012 BRIT Awards**

Best British Single
WINNERS

**2012 Nickelodeon's Kids' Choice Awards**

Best UK Band
WINNERS
Best UK Newcomer
WINNERS

**2011 4Music Awards**

Best Group
WINNERS
Best Breakthrough
WINNERS
Best Video
WINNERS